RACING
CHARACTERS

JOHN IRELAND'S
RACING
CHARACTERS

TEXT BY JULIAN WILSON

Macdonald
Queen Anne Press

Queen Anne Press

First published in Great Britain in 1988 by Queen Anne Press, a division of
Macdonald & Co (Publishers) Ltd
3rd Floor, Greater London House, Hampstead Road, London NW1 7QX

A member of Maxwell Pergamon Publishing Corporation plc

British Library Cataloguing in Publication Data

Wilson, Julian
Racing characters.
1. Flat racing. Jockeys – Biographies
I. Title
798.4′3′0922

ISBN 0-356-17159-0

Made by Lennard Books Ltd
92 Hastings Street
Luton Beds LU1 5BH

Editor Michael Leitch
Designed by Pocknell & Co
Typeset by Jigsaw Graphics
Printed and bound in Great Britain by
Butler & Tanner, Frome, Somerset

CONTENTS

INTRODUCTION

'All men are equal on the Turf – and under it,' said the philosopher. Whilst aspects of the latter part of the epithet are unarguable, I have always viewed the basic precept with misgivings.

Not so John Ireland. His perceptive, penetrative and sometimes savage drawings are composed without fear or favour. Happily his reaction to the sport is ultimately benign!

Horse racing as an industry is an intricate pile of cards always in danger of collapse. The two foundation stones are the Jockey Club, who administer it, and the Owners who finance it.

Everyone in, or around, racing is partly or wholly dependent upon these two groups . . . artists, auctioneers, bloodstock agents, bookmakers, breeders, equine suppliers, farriers, insurers, jockeys, journalists, officials, photographers, stable lads, transporters, trainers, valets, vets and video companies.

Almost without exception, the above individuals are financed by the Racehorse Owner. It would be agreeable if he were to be accorded due deference and respect. Because, however, £25 million is levied compulsorily from bookmakers' profits from the several *billion* pounds bet on horses each year, it is suggested that 'the punter' is financing racing and that the whole show should be arranged for his benefit. The conflicting views on this issue ensure that the framework of racing will continue to represent a battle between 'Them and Us'.

Racing is rich in characters, by its very nature. It is a sport where a sprained tendon or a broken bone can affect the destiny of millions of pounds. Bankers and businessmen learn quickly that racing is never a game of percentages. A virus, a drought, a snowstorm or a Stewards' decision can undo the work of months and years.

Nor is backing horses any less hazardous than owning or training them. When your luck is out, there is no limit to the depth of the pit. Once, in the early Sixties, while I was 'resting' and attempting to exist as a semi-professional backer, I travelled to Wye Races with my last £10 in the world to invest on a novice chaser for whom I had high regard. The odds were 5–1.

The horse jumped immaculately, negotiated the last fence three lengths clear, and my problems seemed for a brief moment at an end. At this same moment another horse who had fallen on the first circuit came charging back down the course, cannoned straight into my 'life-saver', and knocked the unfortunate jockey (Michael Scudamore) out of the saddle. Such an episode only occurs to a man at rock bottom!

Racing is full of such incidents and surprises which create 'character'. It is no sport for dull people, or people who enjoy a 'dull' existence.

Whilst owners are the cog of racing, there are, of course, 'owners' and 'owners'. The 'good owner' pays his bills on the dot; visits the stable no more than once a month, displaying munificent generosity; and accedes to his trainer's wishes to race his horse at Carlisle (the trainer having a soft spot for the cuisine at nearby Sharrow Bay).

The 'bad owner' requires Jockey X to ride his horse in place of the stable jockey; complains at the horse's condition and performance; pays once every six months, under threat; and eventually removes the beast to Trainer Y.

The relationship between owner and trainer is a sensitive mechanism. The skilful trainer achieves total compliance from the owner with all his wishes, whilst conveying the impression that it was all his (the owner's) idea in the first place.

Some owners, however, are not so easily led. A well-known Newmarket character trained for a Jockey Club member who dreaded the prospect of his horses actually *running* because of the expense. One Sunday morning the trainer telephoned the owner:

'Good morning, sir. I'd like to enter your filly at Wolverhampton'. 'Don't do that, I would rather die than be seen at Wolverhampton,' was the reply.

The following week the trainer telephoned again. 'I'd like to enter your filly at Hamilton Park, sir – there's a race she should definitely win there.' 'Don't do that, I would rather my horse died than be seen at Hamilton,' came the reply.

—————

Soon afterwards the filly began to please the trainer and he telephoned the owner. 'Sir, I would like to enter your filly for the Oaks. The entry fee is £200.' There was a brief silence. 'Don't do that, my boy. You know the traffic is terrible leaving Epsom on Oaks Day . . .'

Trainers are now a very different species to 50 years ago. Even then many were still regarded as 'training grooms'. Nowadays, several are millionaires, through the ownership of breeding rights to Classic winners, or the sale of a stable to Arab owners.

Jockeys, likewise, are no longer the forelock-touchers of old. They too have their millionaire set, the most notable of whom has regrettably spent the year 'away'. In a memorable social commentary on TV recently, Lord Howard de Walden observed: 'Oh yes, they (jockeys) are frightfully grand nowadays. They express opinions and things!'

Even the Fourth Estate, in the guise of TV commentators, are now permitted to 'express an opinion'. Twenty years ago an 'opinion' would elicit a tap on the shoulder from a Jockey Club member, and a 'quiet word'.

In fact the modern jockey, notably Cauthen and Asmussen, is so erudite, worldly-wise and socially aware that he could switch comfortably to a career in diplomacy. A far cry from the old-timer living on memories in the Newmarket public bar.

Racing characters come and go. Some go to the wall; some – as we've seen – go to gaol. The characters in this book are 'stayers', all part of the rich patchwork of the Sport of Kings.

IRELAND

—————

Bill Shoemaker is the genuine object – a legend in his lifetime. Incredibly, 1988 was his 40th year as a top-class jockey. Unlike Piggott, he has left no records intact. He beat them all years ago.

It was back in 1970 that he beat Johnny Longden's record of 6,032 winners. Now he is approaching 9,000 winners. He has won over $100,000,000 in stake money and 10 times been top US rider for money won.

At 56 he seems indestructible. But he was always unique. Born at El Paso, Texas, 'Shoe' was so tiny and sickly at birth, he was incubated in an old shoe-box, hence the name-that-stuck. At 7st (or 98 lb), he was always 20 lb lighter than his European counterpart, Lester Piggott, while his tiny legs – no more than a foot from the knee down – made his balance and control inexplicable.

In 1953 he rode what was, at the time, a world-record 485 winners in a year. Steve Cauthen wasn't born for another seven years!

He started riding at Hollywood Park in 1949, and rode 219 winners that year. Since then he has been top rider 18 times at Hollywood.

His worst accident came 20 years ago. A horse fell with him on a muddy track at Santa Anita, breaking his pelvis, and it was feared he would never ride again. The following year he was back, only to have a horse tip over in the paddock at Hollywood Park. That kept him on the sidelines for a further six months.

How rich he is, is anyone's guess, although 10% of $100 million is no small potatoes. Alimony has bitten savagely into his wealth, but 'The Shoe' has backed a winner in current wife Cindy, a statuesque blonde of stunning good looks. Cindy, and a filmstar's house in Beverley Hills, keep the pep in his step.

Like Old Father Thames, he just keeps rollin' on. . . .

WILLIE SHOEMAKER

Barry Hills has not only achieved the success his hard work and keen-wittedness deserve, he has enjoyed every moment of it.

There are those who raise themselves from the grass roots of sport, or industry, who are totally ill-equipped to reap the rewards. Not Barry Hills. He drinks the finest champagne, smokes the best cigars; enjoys Caribbean holidays, stays in the finest houses, and plays backgammon until the early hours. He has a beautiful, rich wife and is master of one of Europe's finest training estates. He also has innumerable loyal friends.

A man who started his racing life as a 10-shilling-a-week apprentice, sleeping in a barn infested with vermin, he is entitled to feel a sense of satisfaction. Barry has an easy manner, and a natural extemporary ability to do the right thing. He would rarely miss out on a good party. On the other hand he would always be out of bed and back home in time for 'first lot'.

Barry is one of the few contemporary top trainers who enjoys a bet. Indeed his success is largely based on betting. His first major *coup* was on a horse called Frankincense in the 1968 Lincoln Handicap when he was travelling head lad to John Oxley. His earnings from this gamble enabled him to start training the following year. He also won many thousands of pounds when Rheingold won the Prix de l'Arc de Triomphe in 1973.

Barry has five sons, three by his first wife Maureen (including twins Michael and Richard) and two by Penny. He is companionable, if occasionally irascible with his staff. Above all, he serves an extremely fine glass of champagne.

BARRY HILLS

Willie Carson, born in Stirling, has all the characteristics of a gritty, obstinate Scots Terrier. Both in a race and in an argument, he pumps and pounds away like a dog defending and grinding away at a juicy bone.

His career has been a triumph. Riding for over 20 years at 7 st 9 lb, he is probably the strongest rider pound-for-pound this century. Certainly, in my lifetime, only Doug Smith had comparable strength, although I never saw Tommy Weston in the saddle.

Early in Willie's career he was in danger of being classified a 'light-weight'. It was an upsetting blow when, as Bernard Van Cutsem's stable rider, he was passed over in favour of Lester Piggott to ride Crowned Prince. To his credit he quickly emerged as a Classic jockey and after a heart-breaking hairsbreadth defeat on Hot Grove, won the Derby on Troy and Henbit in successive years.

The following year was the watershed in Willie's life. A terrifying, bone-crushing fall on Silken Knot in the 1981 Yorkshire Oaks not only cost him his fifth Jockey's Championship, but also, in my opinion, changed his persona. Willie became more introspective, and occasionally morose. A split with his secretary, Ted Ely, had a non-beneficial effect on his career, and as outside rides fell away Willie, quite wrongly, began to believe that his talents were underrated.

A further upsetting influence was the tragic accident to his retainer and friend Major Dick Hern, who was paralyzed in a riding accident. Ironically, at much the same time, the stable struck a disappointing patch. In 1987, Willie's total of winners dropped from 130 to 100, although they included Classic successes on Don't Forget Me.

Willie has much in which to rejoice. He has a devoted wife in Elaine and a fine estate and stud farm at Barnsley near Cirencester. This year's Classic aspirant Minster Son was bred on the stud. Furthermore, Willie's weight enables him to eat what he likes.

The public adore him and his laughter is infectious. Above all, Willie's friends hope that once again he will become a championship contender. He is not much good at being a 'former champion'.

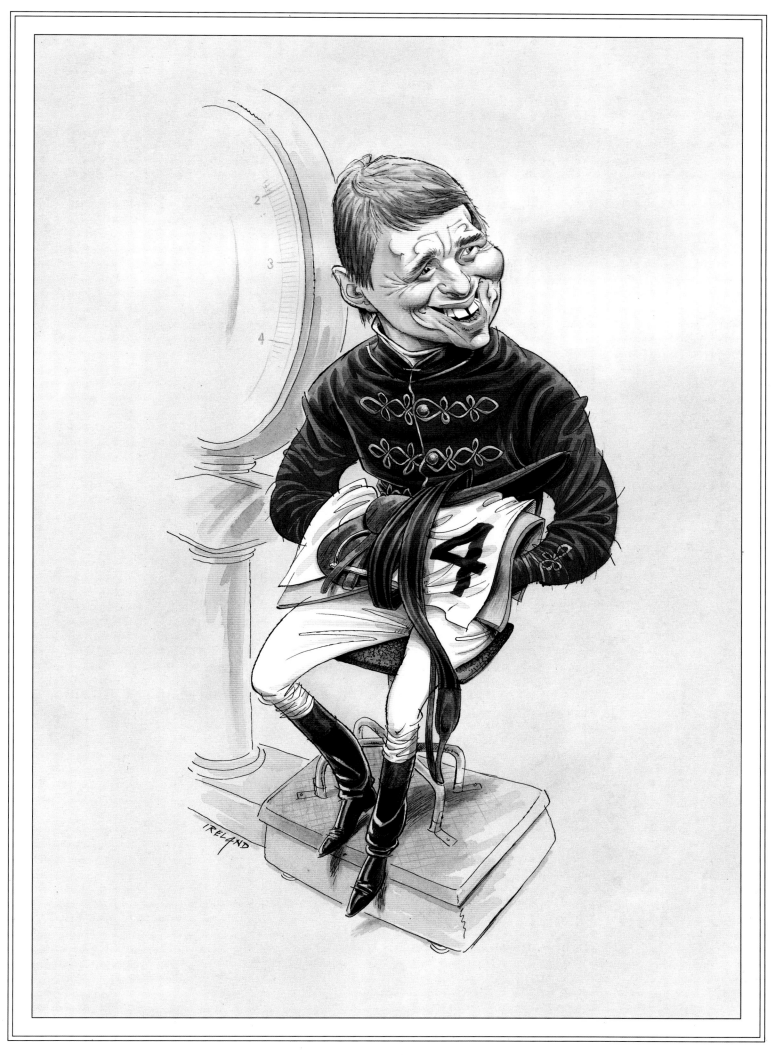

WILLIE CARSON

H M The Queen has won every Classic race on the Flat, except for the Derby. Whatever her triumphs in the fields of diplomacy, humanity and statesmanship, I suspect she will die a truly fulfilled person only if she wins the Derby.

The Queen has 25 brood mares and 34 horses in training, at the last count. The stallions, Bustino and Shirley Heights, stand at the Royal Studs. Her Majesty's Racing Manager is the Earl of Carnarvon, and her Stud Manager is Michael Oswald. Their ultimate ambition is simple: to breed and campaign a horse to win the Derby, or, as a sound alternative, to win at Royal Ascot.

Pall Mall won the 2000 Guineas in 1958; Highclere the 1000 Guineas and French Oaks in 1974; and Dunfermline the Oaks and St Leger in 1977. But the Derby remains elusive. Aureole – second to Pinza in 1953 (Coronation Year) – came closest.

The Queen takes a very positive interest in the mating of her mares, and her racing strategy. She names the yearlings, and visits the Royal stables whenever possible, usually on a Saturday morning.

For over 30 years the *Sporting Life* has been her first-choice newspaper, although nowadays I suspect she prefers the *Racing Post*. Her trainers, Major Dick Hern, Ian Balding, and Balding's brother-in-law William Hastings-Bass, try their very hardest to 'deliver the goods', but the competition of the Maktoum family is extremely fierce.

The Queen has won over 400 races, but her chances of winning the big one are receding.

HM THE QUEEN

Robert Sangster was the first man in Britain to turn horse racing into a major international business. Luckily for his friends, however, he has never allowed business to get irretrievably in the way of pleasure.

His hospitality, *joie de vivre* and innate sense of fun make a day's racing in his company hugely enjoyable. Accessories like vintage Dom Perignon, cold lobster, strawberries and private boxes, not to mention his beautiful wife Susan (Mark II) add to the enjoyment of his society.

Sangster is a fun person. He adores a tilt at the ring, the company of friends and celebrities, and luxurious surroundings. Having recently sold the family business, Vernons Pools, for £90 million, there is every reason to believe that he will continue to enjoy these luxuries.

Sangster's racing empire was built with the aid of Vincent O'Brien and Vincent's son-in-law, John Magnier, in Co Tipperary, Ireland. The strategy was for O'Brien to buy well-bred yearlings with perfect conformation at the Keeneland Sales; train them to win European Classic races, and sell them back to the Americans as stallions for sums of up to $40 million.

In general the operation was extremely successful . . . until the Maktoums. Suddenly Sangster was faced with formidable rivals with equal, if not superior, purchasing power. Yearlings that had cost $2–3 million, were suddenly forced up to $10 million. On the racecourse, the Maktoum horses were increasingly difficult to beat. Classic wins dried up; investment substantially exceeded income. Hence the sale of Vernons Pools.

Through it all Sangster plays on like the band on the *Titanic*. Luckily, thanks to Vernons, the ship is still afloat.

ROBERT SANGSTER

L ester Piggott in the saddle was a combination of Fred Archer, Croesus, and Svengali. At his peak his talent was matched only by his wealth. He was a genius, but flawed.

Piggott dominated and dictated race-riding in a way which only a handful of individuals have ever done. He was lightning-fast from the starting gate (latterly stalls); always perfectly placed throughout a race; and stronger than any of his rivals in a finish.

His Svengali nature enabled him to dictate a pace which suited him and nobody else. If Lester wanted the lead only a fool would dispute it. Retribution would follow; the mistake would not be repeated.

During a race Lester would see openings seconds before they occurred and be ready to pounce. In the finish he perfected the use of the whip to such a degree that he extracted the last ounce of effort whilst keeping his mount perfectly balanced. Nor, latterly, was any lasting damage inflicted.

Hard of hearing, affected by a speech impediment, and unable to eat normally for 30 years, Lester was short on social graces, and was largely content with his own company. Action and achievement, and the consequent rewards, were the adrenalin that kept his body functioning. When a prison sentence cut off this daily 'fix', his life and body began to disintegrate.

How rich was Lester before the Inland Revenue clawed their due? Estimates varied between £10 million and £20 million.

Racing reveres him as one of the three all-time greats. Fred Archer shot himself, Sir Gordon Richards died peacefully a national hero. Lester's future, as ever, remains impossible to predict.

LESTER PIGGOTT

Vincent O'Brien is a perfectionist. His belief in attention to detail has made him Europe's most successful post-war trainer, and a very rich man.

To have won six Derbys in 21 years is remarkable enough. To have won three successive Champion Hurdles, three successive Gold Cups, and then three successive Grand Nationals is staggering beyond belief.

Vincent is strong on strategy. He hates to make a faulty judgment and is meticulous in race-planning and shielding horses from a damaging experience. A pioneer in purchasing American-breds and in particular the off-spring of Northern Dancer, Vincent was faced with the conflict of having top-of-the-ground horses in Europe's wettest country.

His many changes of plan in response to variable weather would infuriate Lester Piggott, an equally meticulous planner. But Vincent hated to risk a horse on ground that could damage him. So horses would be withdrawn, jockeys' journeys were in vain, and trainers whose horses had been 'frightened off' would fume with impotence. For Vincent, it was always the horse that came first.

One of the turning points of his life came when Jack Mulcahy, a likeable Irish patriot who made his fortune in American industry, suggested to Vincent that he insist on owning a 10% share in each horse he trained. Several stallions later Vincent was a multi-millionaire and, despite the occasional financial traumas, he remains very rich.

He is devoted to his Australian-born photographer wife Jacqueline, while his elder son David's achievement in saddling Secreto to win the Derby – at the expense of Vincent's El Gran Senor – gave him great pride.

A modest, private, sensitive man, Vincent has been worrying about life and horses for 45 years. In the meantime he has become a legend.

VINCENT O'BRIEN

P at Eddery, in the saddle, has the good fortune to be a natural genius. Unlike Piggott, he is the right weight, the right shape, and he has a natural affinity with horses.

Skills and complicated manoeuvres that take lesser mortals months and years to master, come to him quite naturally. He looks part of a horse, and achieves with his mount the mutual confidence of the true horseman.

Eddery, like Piggott, was born to it. One of 13 children (four of them professional jockeys) sired by the former Irish jockey Jimmy Eddery, he was dispatched from Ireland at the age of 15 to the late 'Frenchy' Nicholson's 'Jockeys' Academy' at Cheltenham. There he learnt self-discipline, Englishness, and allowed his natural talent to be moulded into a perfect technique. He always appeared the obvious successor to Piggott and went through several of the Great Man's phases, e.g. extreme determination, manifested by reckless riding.

For an Irishman he is by no means gifted with outstanding eloquence, nor has his judgment of the form book made his family and friends rich beyond the dreams of avarice. His timing and temperament, however, are impeccable, and he possesses the enviable ability to fall quietly asleep in the midst of turmoil. He can hold his own with the best at an all-night party and ride as if inspired the following day.

His battles with Steve Cauthen in the past two seasons have lifted the art of jockeyship to its highest level to the delight of all who appreciate sheer genius. Aided by his brother-in-law, Terry Ellis, as secretary and driver, and adored by his devoted wife Carolyn, he is a very fortunate man indeed.

PAT EDDERY

Horse racing, especially at Newmarket, is full of cliques and dynasties. When the author arrived in Newmarket in 1960, the community was still dominated by families such as the Waughs, Leaders and Jarvises. The Press were provided grudgingly with probable runners and glared at across the road from the Limekilns.

Admission to the Newmarket Members' Enclosure was by voucher only – signed by a member – and the idea of someone of stable-lad status holding a licence to train was unthinkable. Against this background Michael Stoute travelled from Barbados, learned his trade, and within 15 years became one of the new Newmarket aristocracy.

Stoute, the son of Barbados's Chief of Police, developed his interest in the Sport of Kings through climbing over the wall to Barbados's Garrison Savannah racecourse at an early age. The horses and their early morning exercise (5.30 am) fascinated him. While still at school, he became a race commentator on Radio Barbados, and his first job application on arrival in England was for the position of BBC TV Racing Correspondent!

Luckily for all concerned, he failed in that ambition, and within seven years he was established as a licensed trainer in Newmarket. He has never looked back.

Stoute is very Bajan in character. He loves cricket, and a day out with the boys, with a few beers. He has a keen sense of humour, self-effacing in every area except racing matters. Racing is business, and not to be taken lightly. Stoute likes to be No 1 and his determination to overthrow Henry Cecil is overwhelming. He laughs long and loud in moments of fun, but withdraws into introspective silence when problems arise.

He sees his role as captain of a successful team, and chooses to share the stable's glory. When Shergar won the Derby, he excused himself politely from the Aga Khan's West End celebrations to return home to his family and staff.

Stoute is not liable to seduction by smart society, beautiful women, cordon bleu food, and vintage wines. His tastes are simple. He just wants to win.

MICHAEL STOUTE

Walter Swinburn, at 26, still has the look of an angel. Walter is not an angel. He was, though, bred to racing and riding. His father, Wally, was a top rider for almost 25 years, winning the Ebor Handicap on By Thunder (6 st 12 lb) in 1954, at the age of 17; and becoming Champion Jockey of Ireland, with a record 101 winners, at the age of 40.

His mother, formerly Doreen Cash, comes from a well-known Irish riding and dealing family. Walter was brought up in England, France and Ireland progressively. A superb allrounder, he was a scrum-half of schoolboy international standard and an accomplished soccer player before race-riding became his business.

Apprenticed to the legendary 'Frenchy' Nicholson and, latterly, to the superbly tutorial Reg Hollinshead, Walter secured the job as stable jockey to Michael Stoute at the age of 19. Within 12 months he had won the Derby on one of the great post-war middle-distance horses, Shergar.

Newmarket is not the easiest community into which a young man can become comfortably integrated. There are temptations and bad influences. In the spring and autumn there are long evenings, money to spend, and passably attractive girls readily available.

It was greatly to Walter's good fortune that he had, first of all, the warmly custodial influence of his landlady, Lottie Dickson, and then the constraining influence of his family, now local stud-farmers, to stabilize him. Despite these beneficial restraints, Walter has nonetheless managed to dispose violently of three Mercedes motor-cars and lose his driving licence (for two years). Nonetheless, his riding remains of the highest quality, notably on the big occasion.

Walter is as brave as a lion. His favourite pursuits are fox-hunting, cricket, ski-ing, and riding the Cresta Run in St Moritz. Arguably his greatest sporting achievement was a bowling analysis of 4–36 for a Newmarket XI against Sir Garfield Sobers' XI at the Kensington Oval, Barbados. His victims included Sobers, Seymour Nurse and Peter Lashley. No-one could recall any bowler bagging the three great batsmen previously in the same innings.

Walter loves a challenge.

WALTER SWINBURN

Although Prince Khaled has been one of Britain's leading owners for over a decade, he remains one of the 'mystery men' of the Turf. A multimillionaire close to the Saudi Arabian throne, he is said to have businesses in Saudi and investments worldwide. But little is publicly known of his professional or private life. He seldom, if ever, gives interviews and prefers his agents to represent him on formal occasions.

It was the former trainer Humphrey Cottrill who introduced him to British racing in 1977. Jeremy Tree had charge of his early horses and remains his No 1 trainer and close friend. Ron Smyth was another pioneer trainer and Prince Khaled has remained loyal to the Epsom veteran, now in his 73rd year.

Known Fact, in 1980, was Prince Khaled's first Classic winner (on the controversial disqualification of Nureyev), and in 1981 he bought and developed the Juddmonte Stud, near Henley-on-Thames, to accommodate his Guineas winner as a stallion. Now his Juddmonte Farms incorporate the original stud; Banstead Manor, a 370-acre stud near Newmarket; Dullingham Stud, a stallion station just five miles away; and Juddmonte Farms Inc., Lexington, Kentucky, a complex of three studs incorporating 3,000 acres.

He has 130 horses in training in Britain, divided amongst six trainers; 60 in France, shared between André Fabre and Criquette Head; and 30 in America with John Gosden and Peter Johnson. He has homes in Saudi Arabia, London, Newmarket and Kentucky. Despite his ubiquitous lifestyle he remains in daily contact with his advisers.

His delight in ownership of Dancing Brave was diminished briefly by his defeat in the Derby and more lastingly by nagging concern over his inconsistent health. The great colt had barely completed his first season at stud before being struck down by the little known Marie's Disease. At the time of writing his future remains uncertain.

For all his reserved exterior, Prince Khaled is said to suffer deeply at the whims of ill-fortune. Nonetheless he remains a good friend and warm host to the few who really know him.

PRINCE KHALED ABDULLA

B ill Gredley is one of the genuine eccentrics of the racing world. Owner of Stetchworth House near Newmarket and the accompanying stud – one of the six finest in Britain – he is very much the 1980s country squire.

Hair tied with a rubber band and informally attired, he holds court in the elegant former home of the Dukes of Sutherland, now garlanded wall to wall with a striking mixture of masterpieces ancient and modern.

A multi-millionaire through property, Gredley owns 30-odd horses in training and as many brood mares, but his approach to the sport is essentially whimsical. Trainers who wish to run Gredley's horses at Catterick, or points further north, rather than Sandown Park, do not find favour. Trainers who serve Taittinger Comtes de Champagne (preferably a vintage prior to 1976) earn unqualified approval.

A host of unparalleled energy and generosity, and boasting the largest and most active ice bucket outside of an Italian restaurant, Gredley takes great delight in mellowing his guests to a condition which invokes fury in wives. At other times he displays a sharp racing brain, and considerable vision.

His close friends include Clive Brittain, Robert Armstrong, Barry Hills (all trainers), Robert Sangster and Steve Cauthen (a tenant). Whether or not Gredley is able to achieve the racing and breeding success that his investment merits remains to be seen. But he will always be able to say, 'I did it my way.'

BILL GREDLEY

H enry Cecil is, above all, a dilettante. Most sportsmen are straightforward, uncomplicated characters, totally obsessed with their own sport. Cecil is the opposite. For a start, he is far from obsessed with racing. If he has no runners, he does not go. If he's at the races, and has no further runners, he goes straight home.

He has no race glasses, and is interested in scarcely anyone's horses except his own. He is, however, fiercely competitive and loves to win.

There is a strong streak of 'Cecil' in his make-up. He enjoys witty conversation and bright extravagant clothes, preferably bought in Italy. He cultivates roses, and adores travelling – Florence and Venice are special favourites.

He was motivated by the success of his step-father, Captain Sir Cecil Boyd-Rochfort, and his father-in-law, Sir Noel Murless, two of the greatest post-war trainers. Henry, acutely sensitive, was conscious of the inevitable comparisons when he took over first his step-father's horses and, latterly, his father-in-law's stables. He was irked by the envy, and suggestions of privilege. He was determined to succeed to such a degree that Sir Cecil should be described as 'Henry Cecil's step-father'.

His twin brother David – for many years they were indistinguishable – wilted under the pressure and dropped out. Henry went from strength to strength. As a teetotal workaholic, he has earned his success.

Cecil is deeply attached to his horses, although he is inclined to be hard on them. He does not encourage sloppiness or laziness in horse or human.

He is a keen observer of humanity. Self-effacing in success, he treads a narrow tightrope between professional responsibility and gentle fun-making. One feels that he is enjoying a private joke which none of us truly understands.

Above all kind and compassionate, he inspires loyalty as well as admiration. That rare thing among successful men, he has made very few, if any, enemies on the way.

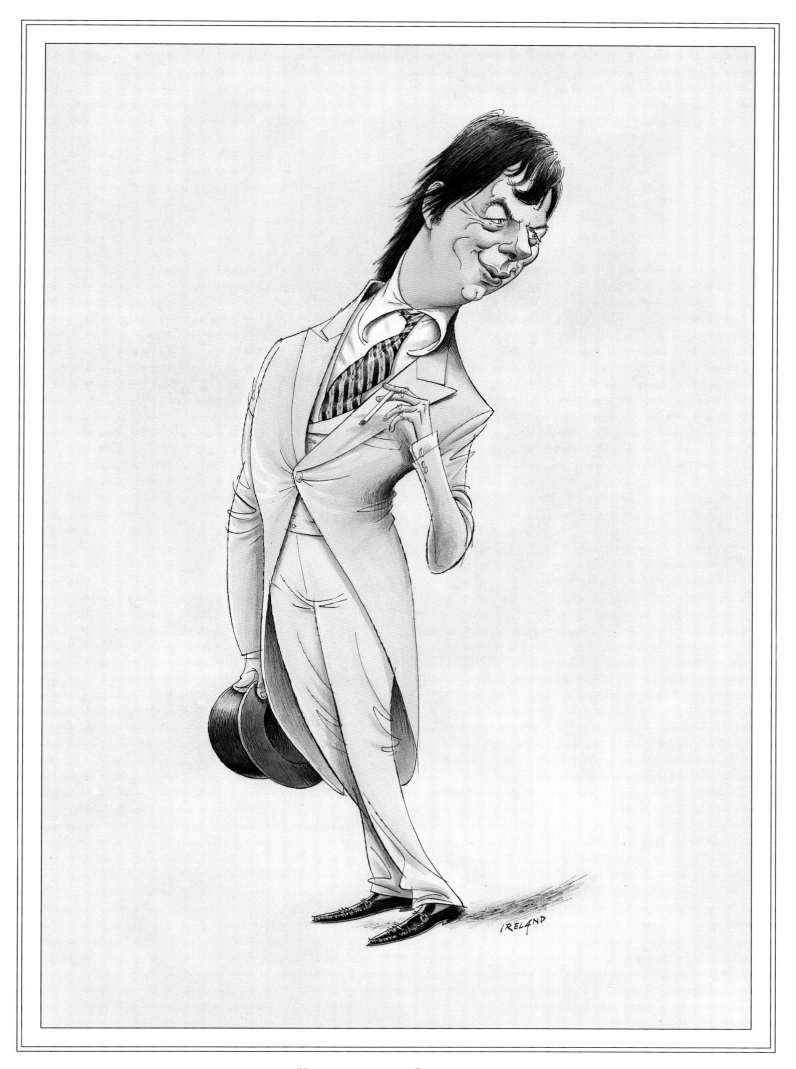

HENRY CECIL

Greville Starkey, 48, is the Peter Pan of racing. Known as 'The Barker' in acknowledgment of his remarkable mimicry of a Jack Russell terrier, he can entertain a racing gathering until tears of laughter course down their cheeks.

Greville's most infamous exploit was the delaying of a trans-Atlantic jet whilst a stewardess and several passengers searched unavailingly for a loose dog. His mimicry of such diverse characters as Lester Piggott, Barry Hills, Henry Cecil and the late Ryan Price – these are collectors' items.

He can also ride. At his peak, in the late Seventies and early Eighties, he was as fine a horseman/jockey as any man riding. Sadly he rode for me once only. It was on a winner.

Always a classic big-race rider, his association with Guy Harwood yielded most of his finest wins. To-Agori-Mou and Dancing Brave won the 2000 Guineas. Unhappily, Dancing Brave's defeat in the Derby created the only disharmony of a long relationship.

Greville is not everyone's cup of tea. His habit of driving a pony and trap over Worlington Golf Course did not endear him to all the members. Nor did his habit, in a race, of casting long, contemptuous looks over his shoulder at floundering opposition endear him to the purists. Above all, his rivalry with Pat Eddery, which came to a head in the contentious battles between King's Lake and To-Agori-Mou, threatened to create an international incident.

For all that nonsense Greville, who rode his first winner in 1955, remains one of the best riders of my lifetime never to become champion jockey.

GREVILLE STARKEY

▬▬▬▬▬▬

L uca Cumani is one of those infuriating foreigners who speak English better than the English. He also has considerable charm, impeccable manners, and a beautiful (English) wife. In the circumstances itis scarcely surprising that he has quickly become one of the country's leading trainers.

Luca was born to horses and racing. His father was a successful trainer, and he himself was Italy's champion amateur rider. He is mellower than the average Italian male, but has Italian machismo in large supply. Until beautiful Sara captured him, there were many young broken hearts suffering intense pain. The more forcible their rejection, the deeper their affection appeared to grow.

It was appropriate, therefore, that his earlier training successes were with fillies. The colts came later, notably Tolomeo, Bairn, Commanche Run and Kahyasi.

Luca remains an active man, and enjoys active holidays, notably on the ski slopes. He also enjoys two weeks of complete calm on the remote Caribbean island of Mustique. Here, his sole concession to activity is an annual cricket match against the local West Indian XI. Cricket is the one sport at which Luca is not competent.

Luca embarked on his training career with endless patience and a determination not to pre-empt nature. As a result his horses tended to be big, backward and late to develop. In recent years he has become more positive and correspondingly more successful. He is widely respected by fellow professionals.

Above all, Luca possesses acute observation and a quick wit. Not only does he express himself better than many of us – he can also outwit us!

▬▬▬▬▬▬

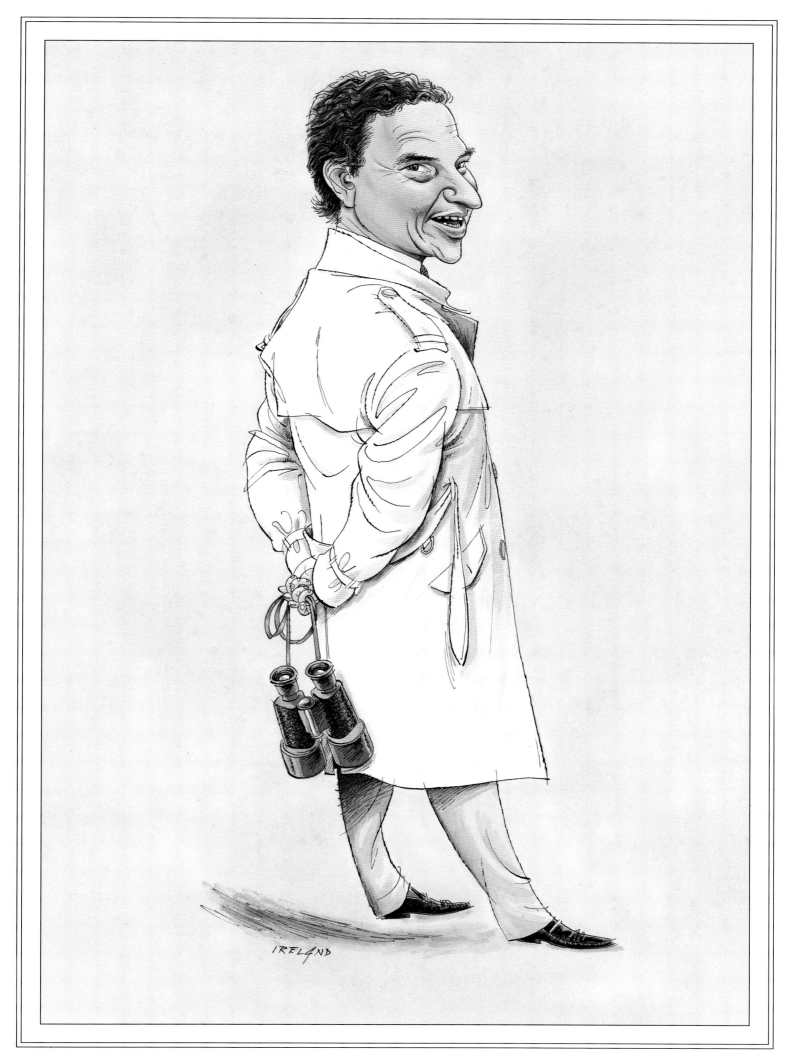

LUCA CUMANI

J oe Mercer is quick, clever, and thinks on his feet. He was a fine and loyal stable jockey to three major stables, and he now has a job as racing manager which he enjoys and to which he is well suited.

For the first 25 years of his life, Joe was 'Manny Mercer's younger brother'. A successful one, mind, winning his first Classic, the Oaks, on Ambiguity, at the age of 18.

Nor was Manny his only brother. There were four sons, and four daughters, in the family. Their father, Emanuel, was a coach painter in the Yorkshire mill city of Bradford.

Manny was the original stylist and everyone's great hero – Joe included. Joe had the brains. Then Manny was killed in a freak accident at Ascot on 26 September 1959. Suddenly Joe was no longer Manny's brother.

Whatever his motivation, Joe became one of the greats. Only three British jockeys – Richards, Piggott and Doug Smith – rode more than his 2,810 winners.

But drama and tragedy always lurked in the background. On the eve of riding his greatest mount, Brigadier Gerard at Royal Ascot, he was involved in a private plane crash that killed the pilot, his friend Graham Cameron. In India, a smuggling charge left Joe with the shame of a prison sentence.

Nor was the business of riding predictable or uneventful. After 23 years as loyal stable jockey to the West Ilsley Stables, the new owner, Sir Arnold Weinstock, sacked him in 1976.

The following four years with Henry Cecil were a vintage era . . . his first jockey's title, at 45 . . . a 1000 Guineas on One In A Million . . . a St Leger on Light Cavalry. But then came a further dramatic parting of the ways, and the tacit question: 'Did he jump, or was he pushed?' All the while Joe remained the most stylish, consistent, dependable jockey riding.

For 'Smokin' Joe', now read 'Gentleman Joe'. He has earned retirement, respect, and what I suspect is considerable wealth.

JOE MERCER

Guy Harwood is a man of exceptional energy and enthusiasm. Always his own man, he has backed his theories with hard cash and come out a big winner.

Guy's background is 'horse power' of a different kind. 'Harwoods of Pulborough' is a big name in the motor trade. His early racing education was with Ryan Price, who 'trained' Guy to ride 14 winners as an amateur.

In 1966 he built the foundations of what has become a 150-horse stable. He was a pioneer of the open American barn in England, a concept pooh-poohed at the time by traditionalists. Indeed, he was regarded as a brash opinionated young man, heading for a fall. Guy stuck to his guns, learned from his occasional mistakes, and gradually built a stable of loyal owners, top-class horses and conscientious staff.

Guy is exceptionally fit. An outstanding ski-er and tennis player, he is also an accomplished opening bat, with the distinction of having hit Sir Garfield Sobers for six over deep mid-wicket at the Kensington Oval!

His energy and hospitality are legendary. Every March he entertains an assortment of racing media to a pre-season display of his best horses, followed by a magnificent buffet lunch, with fine wines. On the first such occasion, he returned from London at 6.30 am after a night in the West End as the guest of some owners; supervised his first lot of horses, and then sparkled in a series of TV interviews.

He is assisted by his daughter Amanda, an accomplished horsewoman, while his second daughter, Gaye, is equally adept. Guy is devoted to his children. With his restless energy, he embodies the spirit of the 1980s. He would also succeed in politics and industry.

GUY HARWOOD

S teve Cauthen is a gentleman and a credit to his profession. It was brave of him to come to England as a fresh-faced 19 year-old to start a second career from the beginning. The easy option was to stay in the United States where, despite a bad run, he could be sure of earning up to a million dollars a year for the foreseeable future.

Instead, the 'Kentucky Kid' arrived at Barry Hills's Lambourn stable, shy, a shade homesick, and facing the unknown. I recall vividly watching him pick through breakfast and then, wearing thin jeans and chaps, vault onto a muscular thoroughbred whose sheer bulk underlined the fragility of Steve's boyish, 8-stone frame.

Until then, in America, he had ridden 'track-work' on pre-programmed, semi-automated, racing machines. Now he faced the wide expanse of Lambourn Downs on an English greenhorn, unused to American-style communication. Steve got through that morning and everything since with charm and style.

It took him six weeks to win his first UK Classic (on Tap On Wood), a little longer to win the Derby, and a shade longer still to become Champion Jockey. It took no time at all, however, for Steve to become hugely popular and a punter's favourite.

Steve has extremely good taste. His three special girlfriends since he came to Britain have been Carolyn Herbert, Franca Vittadini and Annabel Croft. All three are girls men would jump off mountains for.

He lunches at Green's in Mayfair, dines at Pontevecchio in South Kensington and dances at Annabel's. Unhappily, the incompatibility between wining and dining and his chosen craft has imposed certain tiresome restrictions upon his life-style. For all that, Steve remains a delightful companion, and a quite exceptionally good jockey.

STEVE CAUTHEN

Peter Walwyn's bark is very much worse than his bite. Affectionately known as 'Basil' after the appalling anti-hero of *Fawlty Towers*, Peter is a brilliant caricature of himself. His delightful and extremely popular wife 'Bonk' plays the role of Sybil to perfection, except that her efficiency is balanced by long-suffering good humour, and devotion to Peter.

Peter's career as a trainer has been typical of racing's roller-coaster. Champion Trainer in 1974 and 1975, his fortunes ran into a brick wall when the stable was afflicted by equine virus. Senior staff drifted away and his jockey, Pat Eddery, left for rich pickings at Ballydoyle.

Peter felt betrayed, and embraced humility. Now he has played his way back into the first division, snapping at the heels of the new champion generation.

He is a kind man, who enjoys fox-hunting in Leicestershire, and relaxing summer holidays in Majorca with close friends. Always a live wire at a party, he is a showman who leads from the front. He will remember and appreciate a good turn, but woe betide anyone who betrays his trust.

Peter is lucky to have friends who are owners, and owners who are friends, although over a quarter of his horses are owned by Sheik Hamdan al Maktoum. He is an acquired taste, but a good friend to those he cares for.

PETER WALWYN

Prince Karim Aga Khan inherited the role of spiritual leader to the Ismaili sect of Shiah Muslims from his grandfather at the age of 20, in 1957.

His father, Prince Aly Khan, was passed over for the inheritance for reasons personal to Karim's grandfather, but which may have included Prince Aly's liking for gambling, fast women (his wives included Rita Hayworth), and a lifestyle widely considered incompatible with the self-discipline required of the Imam. Sadly, he was killed in a car crash in 1960.

The young Aga Khan was, accordingly, thrust into a role of immense responsibility at a very young age. He also inherited a colossal racing empire at a time when the Sport of Kings was of little interest to him. It says a great deal for his adaptability and perspicacity that he not only maintained the racing and breeding interests, but broadened the base, freshened the blood-lines, and bred one of the great horses of the post-war era in Shergar.

Karim Aga Khan, like his father, is a man of immense charm, and a most generous host, but through no fault of his own liable to attract controversy. His various horse-racing *causes célèbres* have included the financial wrangle with the American Murty brothers over the purchase of the Boussac horses; the 'doping' of Vayraan; and the kidnap and slaughter of the great Shergar.

The Vayraan affair, in which after exhaustive chemical analysis, and extensive legal argument, it was accepted that the horse had 'doped himself', displayed the Aga's immense loyalty to his employees. The Shergar affair, wherein his favourite horse was kidnapped for ransom by a terrorist organization in the mistaken belief that the horse belonged to the Aga, rather than, at the time, a syndicate, was a personal tragedy beyond belief. It was poetic justice that within five years he should have bred two further Derby winners in Shahrastani and Kahyasi.

Nobody's fool, Karim Aga Khan is a man who was dealt a good hand of cards, and has played them well.

H H   A G A   K H A N

Cash Asmussen was christened Brian. At the age of 16, in Texas, his name was changed by deed poll. Ever since, cash has flooded in and Cash does not treat it lightly.

Cash is a big guy for a jockey. He began to stick out like a sore thumb in America where many of the riders came from Mexico and Panama and are in a distinctly smaller mould. So he came to Europe where Piggott and Cauthen made riding at 8 st 7 lb respectable.

To his credit, he became Champion Jockey of France – learning the language, with a little help from a friend, in remarkably quick time – and then contract rider to Robert Sangster and Vincent O'Brien at Ballydoyle. This arrangement did not work so well and Cash returned to France to ride for André Fabre, whose 200 horses include the top-class miler, Soviet Star. With every move, Cash's bank balance has become substantially healthier.

Cash is extremely companionable. He is chatty, intelligent, ambitious. He likes smart clothes, and smart surroundings. He owns an expensive property in London, and whilst in Paris conducts his business from the Bar Anglais at the Hotel Plaza Athénée, picking at sweetmeats and a little caviar all the while. He seems resigned to a limited riding career because of his weight, and is determined to make the most of it. He certainly has the wherewithal to become a successful trainer when he loses the battle with *avoirdupois*.

Cash will always be a favourite with media 'hacks' because he is bright, lively, erudite and helpful. And the guy can ride.

CASH ASMUSSEN

H H Sheik Mohammed bin Rashid al Maktoum and his two elder brothers, Sheik Maktoum and Sheik Hamdan, have taken over racing like a giant steamroller. However, whereas the function of a steamroller is purely destructive, the Maktoums' influence is quite the opposite.

Sheik Mohammed has the highest racing profile. He has almost 400 horses in training worldwide; owns four stud farms and 150 broodmares; and owns, or has major shares in, 15 stallions, including Dancing Brave, Reference Point and Shareef Dancer.

He is a kind and caring man with a deep affection not only for horses, but also for camels and falcons. On a day's camel racing in Dubai, he will have upwards of 50 runners and know each one individually. Top-class camels can change hands for upwards of £¾ million.

Sheik Mohammed is positive and decisive. When he decided recently to build a golf course in Dubai, within months a verdant 18-hole Championship course was constructed complete with clubhouse and irrigation – in the middle of the desert.

Sheik Maktoum, the Deputy Ruler and heir to the Emirate, is the most serious and conservative of the brothers. Conscious of his increasing burden of responsibility – Sheik Rashid has been in ailing health for a number of years – he preserves a most statesmanlike demeanour.

Sheik Hamdan, by contrast, has a great sense of fun. He allocates unintelligible Arab names to his 100-odd horses in training, and laughs heartily at our inability to pronounce them. At home in Dubai, where he is Minister of Finance, he works hard and plays hard, notably at camel racing, hunting with falcons, driving fast cars, and researching electronic gadgets.

He was the first member of the family to make a major impact on British racing. But during 1986 and 1987 his principal trainer Harry Thomson Jones was out of form, and his fortunes waned. His interests broadened and in 1986 he achieved a major coup by winning Australia's Melbourne Cup at the first attempt. His Australian trainer, Colin Hayes, is held in the highest regard by Sheik Hamdan.

Sheik Mohammed stated recently that he and his family would remain involved in British racing 'as long as we are welcome'. They are very welcome.

SHEIK MAKTOUM, SHEIK MOHAMMED, SHEIK HAMDAN

M ichael and Richard are identical twins. They look the same, sound the same, and very often dress the same. Sometimes even their father, Barry, has failed to distinguish between them. Once he booked the wrong one to ride. Rather than take offence at their friends' inability to identify them, the twins tend to enjoy the joke.

Both were apprenticed in Newmarket, and made the most of carefree adolescence. There were stories, perhaps apocryphal, of one twin dating a girl and the other twin taking her out. The possibilities were endless. Several were indeed exploited.

The twins have done extremely well. Richard is now stable jockey to Harry Thomson Jones, whose principal patron is Sheik Hamdan al Maktoum, while Michael is stable jockey to his father, whose main patron is Mr Robert Sangster. These are two excellent jobs and the boys have earned them.

I have always liked Richard and admired his riding. He has ridden for me, and gave the horse a good ride. I know Michael marginally the better because I spent a week in St Moritz with him, ski-ing with Walter Swinburn. Michael was a delightful companion throughout.

Because of this interlude, I am now one of the few people in racing who can differentiate between Michael and Richard. Michael has a small gap between his front teeth. Of course, the trouble is you have to get him to open his mouth. . . . Still, it's a start.

MICHAEL AND RICHARD HILLS

J im Joel, on the threshold of his 94th birthday, is entitled to look back on a varied and colourful life with quiet contentment. Not only has he achieved the rare distinction of winning both the Derby and Grand National, he has also, to his gleeful satisfaction, reached the autumn of his life without succumbing to the manacles of matrimony.

Jim Joel is almost the last of the genuine Edwardians. His first recollection of Epsom on Derby Day is of King Edward VII leading in Minoru in 1909. Joel was 14 at the time.

In World War I he served in France with the 15th Hussars. In 1916 his father, the legendary Jack Barnato Joel, with unaccustomed generosity sent him a racehorse as a charger – a horse called Sirian who had finished second in the Middle Park Plate.

Jim Joel inherited the Childwick Bury Stud – and £5 million – on the death of his father in 1940. He culled the stock, introduced new blood, and brought the declining acreage back to life. But it took him 27 years to breed his first Derby winner, Royal Palace.

The Grand National was an even more elusive target, finally achieved with Maori Venture in 1987. At the time Mr Joel was travelling on a plane from South Africa, where the family's diamond fortune originated.

Yielding to declining eyesight, Mr Joel sold all the broodmares and young stock from his stud in December 1986. It was a terrific wrench. The last yearlings went into training in Autumn 1987. It was the end of a famous dynasty.

Mr Joel is a very kind man. Nothing gives him more pleasure than to entertain racing friends in his box at Newmarket, with a perfectly served glass of champagne – Veuve Clicquot is his special favourite. Nowadays his racing is enjoyed through television, heard more than seen.

He has earned his respect and popularity. His colours have a widespread following, and nowhere more than in the East End of London, where the Joels first came from.

H J (J I M) J O E L

It is very hard to evaluate whether Fred Winter was most successful as a jockey, a trainer, or a human being. As a jockey he was four-times champion, once with a then-record 121 winners. He won the Gold Cup twice, Grand National twice and Champion Hurdle three times.

He was the strongest finisher the author has seen, and ruthlessly determined. His winning ride on Mandarin in the Grand Steeplechase de Paris, when his bridle snapped in the first mile and the horse broke down three from home, is a racing legend. Fred himself was as weak as a kitten after savage wasting and a gastric disorder. Determined to the end he won the following race – the French Triumph Hurdle – on Beaver II.

Yet Fred's career was almost over before it began. He broke his back on his seventh ride over jumps, and confessed: 'I was not all that enamoured with the sport!'

When Fred switched to training in 1964, friends and owners wished him well with misgivings. Within 21 months he had won two Grand Nationals. He was only the second man to ride and train a National winner. In the Seventies he was champion trainer seven years out of eight and regained the title in 1985.

All the while Fred enjoyed life to the full. A reveller till 3 am, Fred would stagger from a party, lost to the world . . . and ride the race of his life the following day.

As a trainer his one blank spot was pre-7.30 am. Woe betide a jockey, stable-lad or visitor who arrived late, or made a pointless remark. John Francome's story of the 'gate that wouldn't open' is a classic of its kind.

For all his bark and bluster Fred is a kind, companionable, family man. His crippling accident in 1987 has damaged the working mechanism, but the steel is still there.

Fred Winter is a legend.

FRED WINTER

HRH The Princess Royal does not suffer fools gladly. She has a waspish wit and a keen determination to excel. Her accomplishment in becoming European Three-Day Event Champion was remarkable for the way she coped with the extra dimension of media pressure.

Insensitive news reporters and contemptible *paparazzi* did their best to breach her iron concentration. They failed, but occasionally The Princess's good humour snapped during practice. Unfairly, she gained a reputation for awkwardness and bad temper. With remarkable self-restraint she continued to do her job and get on with her life. Eventually Fleet Street accepted and respected her for what she is – a hard-working, conscientious and remarkably self-disciplined member of the Royal Family.

The Princess's incursion into horse racing began with a charity race at Epsom in April 1985. She finished fourth, but was hooked. The first win came in August 1986 (on Gulfland at Redcar), and the crowning glory came at Ascot in July 1987 in the Dresden Diamond (Ten No Trumps). Six weeks later the Princess broke new ground by winning a steeplechase on her own horse, Cnoc No Cuille.

The Princess Royal's racing mentor has been the gruff, asthmatic David Nicholson, christened 'The Duke' long before his Royal association. With a little help from his friends, Nicholson has ensured that the Princess has ridden at least *some* horses worthy of her talents. For her part, she has greatly enjoyed the flavour and character of a racing stable and shared the delights and disappointments. Sadly, because of the funeral of family friend Major Hugh Lindsay, the Princess missed Nicholson's finest hour, Charter Party's Cheltenham Gold Cup.

The Princess Royal is brave and able. Long may her interest be maintained.

HRH THE PRINCESS ROYAL

Anyone who does the same job for 50 years is reasonably sure to be very good at it, and almost certainly in love with it. This applies without a doubt to Fulke Walwyn.

Fulke Walwyn is an institution. As a young man with charm, good looks, and a commission in the 9th Lancers, he cut a dashing figure. His name appeared more than once on the dance card of the author's mother at the 1930 Royal Military College Ball!

His twin-sister, Helen, became Mrs Gordon Johnson-Houghton and one of the pioneer lady racehorse trainers, although her career is unchronicled as it was not until 1966 that women were granted licences by the Jockey Club.

Fulke rode as an amateur over fences from 1929–36, and then as a professional. He was champion amateur three times and won the Grand National on Reynoldstown in 1936.

In 1938 he suffered an appalling fall at Ludlow, fracturing his skull for the second time, and remaining unconscious for a month. That was the end of his riding career, and he immediately took out a licence to train. Interrupted only by the war, he has done so ever since.

Fulke has won every major race, and every honour in National Hunt racing. His great horses have included Mill House, Mandarin, Mont Tremblant, The Dikler, Anzio, Taxidermist and many others. In 1973 he became the Queen Mother's trainer and the association has flourished.

Fulke, at 77, retains his charm, together with an acerbic, dry wit. His words nowadays are more carefully chosen, and interjected liberally with 'you knows', but he remains a captivating companion.

His skill with horses, especially bad-legged ones, is indefinable and no-one has a greater talent for preparing a horse for a particular race. Patience, instinct, and the ability to inspire loyalty have served him well.

Fulke, admired and revered by professionals of three generations, is a racing legend.

FULKE WALWYN

P eter Scudamore is a charming, companionable man, with a disarming modesty. When aksed to appear on *A Question of Sport*, he reacted: 'Why do you want me? No-one knows who I am!'

What he is, is a very good Champion Jockey. The charisma of men like Francome and O'Neill is a hard act to follow. Peter is content to be his own man.

Son of a much-admired horseman and jockey, Michael Scudamore, Peter has worked hard at his job, in the modern manner. Very conscious of the effect of the savage injuries sustained by his father and many of his generation, Peter has always tried to avoid unnecessary risks. At the same time he surrenders the 'inner' to no-one and in February 1988 earned a three-week suspension for dispensing instant justice to a younger jockey disputing his *droit de seigneur*.

Peter rode as an amateur whilst training to become an estate agent at Stow-on-the-Wold, Gloucestershire. He rode out nearby for David Nicholson, and 15 months after riding his first winner turned professional and became Nicholson's stable jockey. The partnership thrived until the retirement of John Francome in 1986 led to Peter being offered the plum job as No 1 jockey to Fred Winter. Peter's switch gained him a Champion Hurdle winner with Celtic Shot – but cost him a Gold Cup winner with Charter Party!

Peter, intelligent and erudite, has never lived the profligate, devil-may-care life of his high-flying predecessors. As a jockey he is serious, intense, ambitious, self-critical and determined to win. As a human being he is increasingly laid-back and genuinely interested in life beyond racing.

Peter is a credit to the Scudamore name.

PETER SCUDAMORE

J enny Pitman has done it the hard way. Daughter of a Leicestershire farmer, George Harvey, she was brought up with horses, took the horse-racing path and became a groom for the late Major Geoffrey Champneys.

Here she met a struggling young jockey called Richard Pitman, and married him. The marriage started badly, and eventually got worse. On their honeymoon Richard had yellow jaundice, and was of little use to his eager young bride.

As their marriage matured, so formidable became Jenny's reputation that even the strongest and bravest National Hunt jockeys would throw Richard out of their car after a night out and make a dash for it. When the marriage disintegrated, Jenny's determination to become a trainer became stronger.

After she and Richard had launched a livery yard, the experience encouraged her to go it alone after their inevitable parting. Her resilience, industry and empathy with horses have enabled her to make a colossal success.

History records her remarkable feat in becoming the first woman to train a Grand National winner (Corbiere, 1983) and a Gold Cup winner (Burrough Hill Lad, 1984). At the same time Jenny has become a major personality. Never lost for a quick quip, or a *bon mot*, she is every reporter's and feature writer's dream girl.

Her range of moods include humour, compassion, emotion and contempt. She is fair with the Press, loyal to old friends and supporters, and ever-mindful of the role of the boys in the boiler room. She is, too, a formidable enemy, not always quick to forgive, and disinclined to suffer fools gladly.

A thoroughly liberated woman, Jenny is better to have as a friend than an enemy.

JENNY PITMAN

J onjo O'Neill is almost too good to be true. A kind, quiet man full of
goodness and courtesy, he rode like a demon but remained a gentleman.

Jonjo's life has an almost religious quality. His faith has been tested to
the limit by a succession of crises.

In 1980 he broke his leg so badly at Bangor-on-Dee that amputation was
a real possibility. In 1986, struck down by cancer, his life was in the balance.
In 1988, when his wife Sheila left him, his whole will-to-live was thrown into
question.

Throughout all the turmoils of his life, Jonjo has remained cheerfully
unaffected by self-pity, and a tireless inspiration to the millions who
worship him.

The fourth son of a cobbler in Castletownroche, Co. Cork, Jonjo was
determined from an early age to become a jockey. Each day he would cycle the
14 miles to and from school, to bolster the muscles on his sinewy, 3 ft 6 in,
3½ stone body. Instilled with the need for self-discipline and clean-living by
his authoritarian father, Jonjo has remained a teetotaller throughout his life.

Within five years of arriving in England in 1973, he had become not
only champion jockey but the record-holder for the number of winners in a
season, a remarkable 149. In between the triumphs on Sea Pigeon and
Dawn Run, there were the tragedies of the death of Alverton and his
personal traumas.

What Barry McGuigan has done through boxing, in many ways Jonjo
has accomplished through racing. Quite simply, he is probably the most
likeable man in sport.

JONJO O'NEILL

———

G ee Armytage is a health hazard. Young, blonde, attractive and erudite, she is a rival to turn the head of the most ruthless professional. Luckily, she is marginally less seductive in hair-net and skull cap than in a summer dress with blonde hair billowing. Nonetheless she is not someone to squeeze willingly into the wings.

Gee has no desire to be regarded as a sex object. Her parents were tough; her brother is competitive, and despite her feminine appearance she is far happier as 'one of the boys'. She certainly rides hard – sometimes too hard. Her determination to prove herself led to three fines for excessive use of the whip in her first season.

Friendly tuition from Stan Mellor and a serious talking-to from father (trainer Roddy Armytage) ironed out the excesses. But the determination is stronger than ever, especially after the disappointment of the 1988 Grand National. Here, riding Gee A, she led the field on the second circuit only to pull a shoulder muscle after her mount made an awkward jump, and had to pull up. Uninformed post-race comment that, as a girl, she was not strong enough in the first place, lit the blue touch-paper well and truly!

Of course, Gee's record speaks for itself. The first girl to beat the professionals at the Cheltenham Festival, she had no alternative but to turn professional in an era when 'chippy' inadequates make life awkward for the successful amateur.

Off the racecourse, Gee is less self-assured than on horseback. Berkeley Square and the West End of London are not her natural habitat. She is a girl who would always want to be home in Berkshire by day-break.

Gee is a tough cookie, and very independent. What she will *not* do is end up marrying a National Hunt jockey.

———

GEE ARMYTAGE

D avid Elsworth is a champion trainer, but he has certainly not followed the rose-scented path of his flat-racing counterpart. David has explored the full gamut of racing life. Stable lad . . . claiming jockey . . . assistant trainer to an eventually disqualified person . . . market trader. . . . There were many twists to his controversial life before his ultimate coronation at Liverpool in April 1988.

But even in the year that Rhyme 'N' Reason's Grand National clinched for him the trainer's championship and Desert Orchid won his second 'Racehorse of the Year' award, there was disturbing controversy. Cavvies Clown was found to be harbouring traces of anabolic steroids in *three* post-race dope tests. How did it happen? The mystery was only partially explained.

David has never lost his appetite for hard work, or forfeited his basic racing instincts. These include the pleasure of a 'right touch'.

The writer's first acquaintance with the then-claiming jockey was as owner to jockey in an attempted *coup* on 3 April 1969. The horse in question was 'readied' for a 20–1 gamble in a novice's hurdle at Southwell.

Two things went wrong. A delayed start resulted in the SP dropping from 20–1 to 7–1; and the horse finished second! Elsworth would have received a generous present in the region of £25 in the event of success. Whether the jockey was castigated I cannot recall. But now, in his new exalted status, David delights in haranguing the writer for a word out of place in his TV role!

In Spring 1988, with seasonal prize-money earnings of over £300,000, David could look back with satisfaction on a long climb, with many a slip, but with the summit now in sight.

DAVID ELSWORTH

John Francome is the archetypal modern sporting hero. Rebellious, contentious, and defiant of accepted convention, he delights in taking the alternative path.

If John is 'carded' for a West End party, or invited to dine with rich or distinguished hosts, he will invariably go instead to a Rock concert, or a football match. If John is introduced as one of the great names in National Hunt racing, he will retort: 'Actually I prefer the Flat.' If John is invited to a smart box at Cheltenham, or for a day's hunting in Leicestershire, he will reply: 'Thanks very much, but I would rather play tennis.'

John has immense ability in many directions, but despite his beliefs and unquenchable ambition, he will never display a talent comparable to his riding over fences. A former junior champion showjumper, John could present a horse at a fence with an uncanny accuracy. In the heat of the battle, with whips up, he would measure his mount's stride to total perfection.

It was largely this skill that saved him from serious injury in the most dangerous of all sports. He bowed out at the top, to enjoy life with his full faculties.

Even as a jockey, he could never suppress his rebellious streak. His long, curly, 'gypsy' locks would infuriate his employer, the draconian Fred Winter. He would drive racegoers to apoplexy by riding in a manner suggesting incompetence or dishonesty, and return seemingly without a care. More often than not he was vindicated by subsequent events.

He called the Stewards 'Cabbage Patch Dolls' . . . he was 'warned off' for associating with a bookmaker . . . and featured in a sensational phone-tapping scandal which threatened to incriminate other jockeys. In between these scandals, and moments of silliness, he rode more winners than any other jumping jockey in history.

Life will never be dull for John Francome.

JOHN FRANCOME

From the day in 1949 that Major Peter Cazalet paid £1,000 for a steeplechaser called Monaveen, and registered him in the joint-ownership of Queen Elizabeth and her daughter The Princess Elizabeth, The Queen Mother has been the spirit of National Hunt racing.

It was the late Lord Mildmay, staying at Windsor Castle for the Royal Ascot meeting, who kindled the flame of interest in his hostess's heart. Mildmay had suffered the mortification of losing the 1936 Grand National on Davy Jones through a broken rein and the 1949 National on Cromwell through an attack of cramp.

Little was The Queen Mother to know that within a decade she would suffer the cruellest Grand National defeat of all, the spectacular collapse of Devon Loch within sight of the winning post. Remarkably, all three horses were trained by Cazalet.

From the small beginning with Monaveen, steady and consistent success was to follow. The Royal string grew to around a dozen, and big winners began to appear . . . Manicou (King George VI Chase), Makaldar (Mackeson Hurdle), The Rip (Grand Sefton), Double Star (Gainsborough Chase).

More recent favourites were Escalus, Inch Arran, Game Spirit (21 races), Isle of Man (14 races) and Special Cargo (Whitbread Gold Cup). Through all the success and failure, The Queen Mother has remained sporting and serene, a coveted embellishment to the very heart of the sport. Cheltenham, Newbury and Sandown act as irresistible magnets to the familiar, blue-coated enthusiast. Her presence dignifies and inspires. Every promoter and sponsor covets her patronage.

The Queen Mother has compassion and humour. Some years ago, a Royal runner trained by Cazalet came to the final fence at Kempton in second place. The leader, ridden by another Cazalet jockey, Bruce Gregory, crashed at the last. The Royal runner won.

'Arise, Sir Bruce,' yelled a wag from the Stands.

The Queen Mother enjoyed the joke.

HM QUEEN ELIZABETH THE QUEEN MOTHER

Steve Smith Eccles is the last survivor of the Old Order. In olden days jump jockeys were men of iron . . . hard-riding . . . hard-living . . . hard-loving . . . hard-drinking. They would push their bodies to the limit of its endurance and vie with each other in the pursuit of extremes.

Nowadays there are non-drinkers, percentage men, and celibates. Steve Smith Eccles is none of these.

Steve grew up in a region of Derbyshire where the obvious option was to go down the pit. That was his father's profession. Steve, muscular but under-sized by the standards of coal-mining, opted for another tough apprenticeship – in a Newmarket racing stable.

Tom Jones was the man who moulded Steve into a top-class jumping jockey. For his pains Steve rewarded him by enveigling his daughter (Di Haine) to become his constant companion. Steve would appear to have had the best of both bargains, despite the turbulent nature of the affair.

Steve is brave, determined, and seemingly terrified to allow a day go by unpunished. An enjoyable companion at Sunday lunch, he is not averse to allow lunch to run into tea . . . or supper. Despite that his weight is fairly stable at 10 st 2 lb.

Steve's *cause célèbre* came when Di locked him out of their room over the 1986 Grand National meeting; Steve bedded down in his car; and car and Steve were 'kidnapped' by a local tearaway. The exact dimensions of this episode may never be revealed, but it ensured Steve front-page status in the tabloids on Grand National day. For once he was well aware that he had overstepped the mark.

Steve's riding career will be most remembered for his Champion Hurdle hat-trick on See You Then. His post-racing activities will be remembered by a wide – very wide – circle of female friends.

STEVE SMITH ECCLES

Nick Henderson is a 'good egg'. Born with a silver spoon firmly embedded, he has embraced the principle that the luckiest people are those who work hardest.

A skilful and stylish amateur jockey, Nick submitted to a training apprenticeship with Fred Winter and learnt well. In Summer 1978 he took two major steps – marriage to Diana Thorne (whose father, the late John Thorne, will always be remembered for his epic Grand National ride on Spartan Missile), and the commitment to train horses. Both projects have been a huge success.

Nick manages to combine the all-important qualities of achieving success and having fun. Quite able to hold his own at the legendary 'Lambourn lunches', he remains alert, conscientious, and punctual for 'first lot'.

Owners like Bobby McAlpine, Bill Shand-Kydd, Ivan Straker and Georgina Bronfman embody the spirit of the yard. But the gaiety and enthusiasm are tempered by patience and common-sense. Nick's training of the bad-legged See You Then was a masterpiece of its kind, and the near-miss of The Tsarevitch in the National, after restricted preparation, was a minor miracle.

Nick is long-suffering, helpful to the Press, over-indulgent to occasional tiresome owners, and modest about his achievements. A keen golfer and field sportsman, he enjoys life to the full. At 37 he has many successful years ahead of him.

NICK HENDERSON

Peter O'Sullevan was 70 years old on Thursday 3 March 1988. Two days later he travelled to Haydock Park, delivered his usual impeccable commentary, and returned to London to visit an old friend in hospital, before dining in style in the West End.

O'Sullevan enjoys the good things in life. His elegant Chelsea flat is adorned with fine art, with a conspicuous balance in favour of Skeaping, a very close personal friend until his recent death. He is an explorer of high-class restaurants across Europe and an aficionado of fine wine. He is always a solicitous and entertaining companion.

In December 1967, when racing in Britain was brought to a standstill by an outbreak of foot-and-mouth disease, BBC TV's Sports supremo, Peter Dimmock, boomed down the phone: 'Find me some racing – anywhere!' It was thus that O'Sullevan and I spent Christmas 1967 inthe South of France preparing for racing at Cagnes-sur-Mer on Boxing Day.

The culinary side of the expedition was a triumph. Cocktails on the Promenade des Anglais in Nice; dinner in the Old Town; lunch alfresco on the Port . . . and so on. Unhappily this perfectly managed preparation, interspersed with hours of homework, came to little avail. As David Coleman proudly proclaimed, 'And now – a *Grandstand* exclusive – the first horse-racing televised in Britain for a month . . .' The pictures from Cagnes disappeared from the screen – and that was that!

O'Sullevan has a single-minded, almost ruthless professional approach to his work. Demanding the highest standards from himself, he isintolerant of shortcomings from those around him. Woe betide production staff and technicians who earn his displeasure.

Away from the arena, O'Sullevan is thoughtful and caring. Despite his innate shyness, he seldom refuses a call to conduct charity auctions, and does a great deal of unsung charitable work. It was typical of him, on the morning of this year's Cheltenham Festival, to telephone an ailing colleague to inquire of his health.

O'Sullevan remains incomparable and ageless. Once I asked him when he was going to give the rest of us a chance. 'When I dry up in the middle of a race, it's "Over To You Julian,"' he laughed.

PETER O'SULLEVAN

John McCririck is a disgrace. A disgrace to his school (Harrow), his wife ('The Booby') and his profession. He is undisciplined, unkempt and unabashed. He also appears to be by far the most popular individual on Racing TV.

McCririck was a contemporary of mine at school, although resident in a different house and, to the best of my recollection, in a considerably lower class. His appearance was notable for its quite exceptional untidiness. His tailor had clearly been fighting a losing battle from the outset and he finally surrendered.

His keenest skill was table tennis at which he excelled. He introduced to Harrow the new thick-rubber Chinese table-tennis racket with which he was almost unbeatable.

It never looked like being an easy task for McCririck to find gainful employment and his first career as a trainee hotel catering manager was doomed to failure. Thereafter he flirted with private handicapping, bookmaking, punting, and finally journalism.

He became Coursing Correspondent for the *Sporting Life* which he did extremely well, and betting co-ordinator for BBC Television, lifting this service from mediocrity to excellence. Whether ITV's decision to elevate McCririck to visual prominence was in the interests of aesthetic or cultural excellence is a matter of opinion. What is beyond dispute is that it has made him one of TV Sport's larger-than-life characters, with a substantial cult following.

Beyond all this nonsense, John is an extremely kind and likeable man; despite his appalling vulgarity and indiscretion, it is impossible not to be fond of him, and to forgive him almost anything.

JOHN McCRIRICK

Brough Scott has never been a man to take a leisurely walk if he could possibly run. At 45, his youthful enthusiasm remains unbridled. With an attitude combining the finer qualities of St Paul and Don Quixote, he charges from cause to cause and project to project with an unfathomable, vibrant energy.

He has charged headlong at a variety of targets, and conquered a satisfactory proportion. Certainly he has travelled a long and sometimes arduous path since, towards the end of a successful career as an amateur and professional steeplechase jockey, he asked the writer: 'Do you think there would be something I could do in television?'

After a widely-acclaimed launch on the already well-manned BBC network, Brough was offered the opportunity of a deeper involvement at ITV. He seized the chance, and has never looked back. Frontman and co-ordinator on Channel 4; award-winning *Sunday Times* columnist; newspaper Managing Editor; author; video writer and presenter and tireless charity worker . . . somehow Brough also contrives to be a devoted husband and father of four.

Brough's appeal is largely in his boyish charm. His strong belief has always been the need to broaden the appeal of racing. More than most, he has achieved a satisfactory return with the age-old question: 'How does it *feel* . . . ?'

Above all he has never lost sight of the English gentleman's heritage of duty. In his case, he can be justifiably proud of putting a great deal more into the sport than he ever took out.

BROUGH SCOTT

I n the moment of transcendence, when a man's life flashes before him, the vision of Ayala at his right shoulder will surely return to haunt John Oaksey.

It is ironic that three of racing's great media names – Oaksey, Pitman and Dick Francis – should have experienced the agony of traumatic defeat at Aintree. In Oaksey's case he drew strength from Carrickbeg's last-gasp defeat at the hands of 66–1 Ayala. With the sweat still pouring from his wracked body, he dictated one of the great accounts of the Greatest Steeplechase to the *Sunday Telegraph*.

That, and a thousand other on-the-spot reports, notably Mandarin's heroic triumph in the Grand Steeplechase de Paris, bear testimony to Oaksey's life-long affection for the sport of steeplechasing.

Oaksey, riding for most of his career as The Hon. John Lawrence, was unarguably one of the finest post-war amateur jockeys. It was no doubt a disappointment, if not a surprise, to his father when his son and heir foreswore the legal profession for a career in racing journalism.

John read Politics, Philosophy and Economics at New College, Oxford, and was awarded an exchange fellowship at the Law School at Yale University. But racing and riding had too great a lure for the almost-qualified barrister. Cheltenham, Aintree and Sandown Park became his preferred habitat, and have remained so through 30 years of inspired journalism, and almost as long a period of tele-broadcasting.

Oaksey was always a fierce competitor, and a hard man to beat. A local magistrate, trustee of the Injured Jockey's Fund, and a tireless worker on behalf of racing's work-force, Oaksey, like Brough Scott, has more than repaid his debt to the sport he loves.

LORD OAKSEY

P hil Bull is not a man who inspires affection. He is abrasive and irascible. He has an ill-disguised contempt for amateurs, and intellectual inferiors, amongst whom he appears to include the majority of the opposite sex. He is, in fact, what many would consider the archetypal Yorkshireman.

Bull's principal contribution to Turf history is his foundation of the Portway Press, publishers of *Timeform* and *Racehorses of 19––*. These publications have proved of considerable benefit to amateur, part-time punters, and international bloodstock dealers.

On the other hand they have provided informed comment and opinion to the equal benefit of bookmakers which has rendered the battle with the 'Old Enemy' that little bit more difficult. This writer does not subscribe to *Timeform*, although it must be said that the majority of racing journalists do.

Bull, a graduate of Leeds University, became a Professor of Mathematics and it was his grasp of mathematical probabilities that enabled him, for lengthy periods, to maintain an ascendancy over bookmakers. He achieved success as racing adviser to William Hill, one of the most formidable odds layers of his generation, and he himself bred a number of top-class horses including Romulus.

In his heyday, Bull was a savage critic of the Jockey Club, and what he considered incompetence in the Rules of Racing and their execution – in particular the Rules relating to disqualification. Phil Bull will die a proud and prickly Yorkshireman, but he is mellower now and quite capable of proving an agreeable after-dinner companion.

PHIL BULL